HUMAN
EQUATION

MULTIPLY YOUR MENTAL
AND PHYSICAL POWERS
BY UNDERSTANDING YOURSELF

BY KIRK ELLIS

authorHOUSE®

AuthorHouse™
1663 Liberty Drive
Bloomington, IN 47403
www.authorhouse.com
Phone: 1 (800) 839-8640

Published by AuthorHouse 03/15/2017

ISBN: 978-1-5246-7076-4 (sc)
ISBN: 978-1-5246-7075-7 (e)

Library of Congress Control Number: 2017901857

Print information available on the last page.

Any people depicted in stock imagery provided by Thinkstock are models, and such images are being used for illustrative purposes only. Certain stock imagery © Thinkstock.

This book is printed on acid-free paper.

Because of the dynamic nature of the Internet, any web addresses or links contained in this book may have changed since publication and may no longer be valid. The views expressed in this work are solely those of the author and do not necessarily reflect the views of the publisher, and the publisher hereby disclaims any responsibility for them.

ACKNOWLEDGEMENTS

I would like to express my gratitude to those who helped me in my creation of this book. To Monica Ellis who edited the book. To Doug Pearson, who I used as a sounding board for many of the concepts that I have presented. To Janell Lanse, Nan Ellis, and Quint Ellis for their under - standing and support. To Marvin Giddings for his art work. To Lana Giddings for her artistic lettering abilities. To Richard Myer for his help in describing the picture examples.

The Human Equation

Values x Belief System = Quality of Life

table of contents

INTRODUCTION

Because man is adaptable, creative and educable, he has won control over the scientific endeavors with which he has chosen to be preoccupied. He chose to conquer the material world and did. He provided material comforts so that every one could enjoy a better life. And they do. But this enjoyment is limited. Material possessions, money, power, position, do not eliminate stress, nervousness, fear, anger, anxiety, resentment, envy, jealousy, worry, agitation, and hostility. These intangible forces must be controlled, understood and eliminated before life is enjoyable.

Happiness and adaptability, come from a quality of mind not from the quality of material possessions.

Power, title, position, do not make a good leader. The understanding of human behavior makes a good leader.

Confidence, good judgment, and insight are qualities that are acquired by good thinking habits, not by accident.

Organizations, cultures, and individuals who find enduring success, will be those who elevate the worth of themselves and others, along with their goals and plans.

Man has conquered everything but himself. The final and most important conquest is at hand, the development of our own natural powers. Tapping the strength and wisdom of our own natural moral nature is the final step toward self fulfillment and world peace.

People and society are burdened with many unnecessary problems, because the human potential and natural abilities are not being used. Once people understand their own nature, they can automatically deal with life in a wise, effective, successful manner. By effectively utilizing mental and physical powers, stress, tension, anxiety, fear and worry are eliminated. When man understands himself, he understands life.

Every person is successful to the extent that they understand and utilize the natural laws of mind, body and spirit to their advantage. In everything that you do natural principles operate for or against you, depending upon your own wise use of them. Scientists represent natural phenomina with formulas. The scientific formula is successful to the extent that it relates to the realities of natural law. An individual is successful to the extent that he uses natural laws that apply to human nature. You cannot deviate from the laws of the mind and body any more than you can from gravity. Qualities of life, mental stability, character, personality traits, good leadership, and body power depend upon natural law. These laws are revealed in the HUMAN EQUATION FORMULA.

The human equation is presented and explained in this book. This formula operates for all people, organizations, clubs, and societies.

THE HUMAN EQUATION

Values x Belief System = Your Quality Of Life

$$V \quad x \quad B \quad = \quad Q$$

The equation gives you an in-depth understanding of yourself and provides physical tests, so you will have an opportunity to gain an experiential understanding of your own personal powers.

The superior athlete, the professional manager, the successful individual of the future will be those who learn how to apply the Human Equation successfully.

What we have achieved in our scientific endeavors, so far, is only a prerequisite to the potentials that are possible once the human equation is understood and used constructively within the mainstream of society.

The Human Equation
Values   x   Belief System   =   Quality of Life

Part I

VALUES

Your values determine your way of life, quality of life, personality traits, mental state, motivation and behavior. Your values select and screen incoming information and influence your perception of events. Your life operates according to your own values, this is the KEY to understanding yourself - the path that determines your future happiness.

There are two value catagories, a positive one and a negative one. The values chosen provide a basic framework that determines the stability of the mind and body. Positive values make the mind calm and stable, they also strengthen the power of the body. Negative values disturb the stability of the mind and arouse harsh emotions that act upon the body in such a way that flexibility, coordination and perception are hindered.

Body, mind, and values are related, they function together. Change the values, and the mind and body automatically change. Values play a major role in integrating mind and body into a harmonious relationship. Negative values divide the mind and body relationship - positive values unite mind and body.

Once you are familiar with the dynamics of values, you will know how to strengthen your mental and physical abilities, eliminate stress, tension, and anxiety. You will also acquire ideal personality traits, that will aid you in achieving continuous success.

Values equal your quality of Life

The Human Equation

Values x Belief System = Quality of Life

POSITIVE VALUES

Some of the positive values are: kindness, modesty, discretion, respect, adaptability, impartiality, and empathy. These qualities stimulate feelings of well-being, tolerance, confidence, sympathy and friendship. Insight good judgment and evenmindedness are then cultivated.

Positive values are the qualities of benevolence. By using these type of qualities, moods do not uncontrollably fluctuate. Behavior and emotions become reliable. Personality traits can be trusted. Reliable behavior patterns are established. Courage, psychological endurance, perseverance, fearlessness, firmness, and strength of mind are cultivated. Personal opinion does not waiver because of pressure of threat. Life is faced unhampered by doubt or hesitation.

Qualities such as sympathy, admiration and fairness, strengthen concentration. Agitation is then neutralized. Anxiety and resentment disappear. A general optimism occurs. The body stays relaxed, the ability to adapt, and respond to changing circumstances increases. Flexibility of mind and accurate perception become strong behavior traits. The ability to recover quickly in the face of an upset is acquired.

Fear is also eliminated as discretion, empathy, and restitution increase.

Our body has a concentration of vital life energy, which is located in the area of the hips. Tension, anxiety, and anger move the energy upward, peace of mind will move the energy downward.

Positive values keep the mind in its most stable natural state, so the body energy will increase its intensity downward. Timing, alertness, coordination and perception become quick and accurate. Muscles stay relaxed, tension is reduced, and endurance increased. Pulse and respiration are lowered. Body and mind are in harmony, and body power is at its strongest.

Physical tests with positive values are on page 54

The Human Equation

Values x Belief System = Quality of Life

NEGATIVE VALUES

Negative values include: Envy, greed, jealousy, egotism, revenge, resentment, and anger, these are some of the basic ingredients that cause worry, anxiety, sorrow and trouble. When these values dominate the mind there are inadequate personality flaws such as irrational conduct, perplexity, nervousness, and tension.

Envy, jealousy, greed, combine to stimulate agitation and anger. Negative values such as these react together as a group, creating disequalibrium of mind and body. If negative values become the driving force that directs your every action, you are out of harmony with ongoing events. Heightened impulses interfere with social interactions; patience and thoughtfulness are reduced.

Ill will halts progress in becoming fully human. Because of ill will, reverence for life, idealism, receptivity, become infirm. There is a deficiency in will power. The more time invested in this mode of behavior the stronger the negative emotional patterns become. Grudges and hostility turn into faulty, malajusted behavior patterns. Negative urges emerge automatically, unconsciously, without too much effort, Distructive critical judgment, generate defensive thinking by others. Opportunities are traded for skepticism.

Negative values disturb the natural health of the body. Nerves, muscles, glands, are adversly affected, mind is less adaptable. If the negative impulses are inhibited they cause chronic muscle tensions, and physical ridgidity. Health problems such as ulcers, headaches, tension and depression become daily problems.

Negative values cause tension and anxiety. This negative energy flows upward from the area of the hips, this is why the body balance is lost and coordination of body movements becomes stiff and awkward.

Negative energy tests are on page 54

Values determine your vision

You see from within

Values design your reality

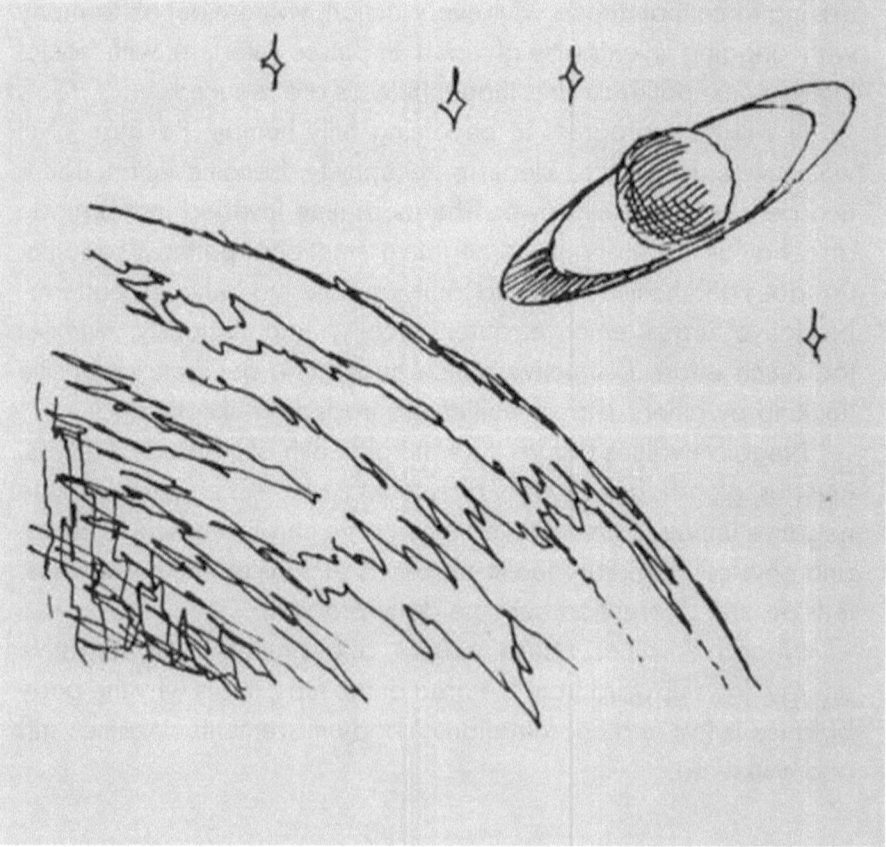

VALUES AND INSIGHT

Perception and insight are based upon modesty, restitude, and discretion. Those who have the best vision

Tolerance and kindness help maintain objectivity when approaching daily problems. Through tolerance and respect there is evenmindedness and impartiality. Then flexibility, buoyancy, and adaptability are added to the personality. With these traits the mind follows change without confusion, frenzy, or emotional overreactions.

Respect, unconditional friendship generate a positive mood; concentration deepens, behavior is temperate and sound. The state of mind stays alert with quick accurate perception.

Compassion, kindness, honesty, and trust, develop a higher degree of understanding yourself and life. By adopting these values, you gain wisdom, do to the fact that you are free from prejudice. You realize that everyone has his faults and strengths, so cooperation with acceptance becomes the rule. When course of action is sincere and honest, the way of life is then guided by clarity of thought. Most specifically you can think for yourself with complete confidence. With a coherent mind you are not at the mercy of overpowering emotions, or at the mercy of group fads. Security, contentment, are found within your own quality of thinking.

Those who see with insight consider the welfare of others, they realize needs and wants immediately as they arise. The mental state that is required for clarity of thought also stimulates feelings of deep compassion. A deeper, wiser, social self is revealed. The urge to be charitable and philanthropic is strong. Instead of being self-centered you become socially integrated. Pride, fear of failure, good, bad, win or lose, self pride, egotistical "I", prejudices and dogmas are absent.

We are born without the knowledge of relationships. We learn to form a connection between the house where we live and the rest of the neighborhood. As we grow older we see a larger view, the house, city, nation and world are seen as a connected whole. As we study physics, chemistry, and biology, we learn to interrelate these subjects. Taking old parts and assimilating them into a new holistic form is important to our ability to understand life better.

Life moves onward when the thought process connects old ideas with new ones, this adds a new dimension to our lives. Maintaining an open enquiring mind, seeking to combine new ideas in a new way, builds insight.

People and cultures often reach a point where they tend to stop forming new relationships and settle down to a set way of thought. This hinders insight.

The beauty of life is to keep expanding, learning, widening and broadening your view of the world. Physics, biology, chemistry, physiology, and religion are now seen as interlinked. We have reached such a high level of understanding that a professional in one field is able to relate his subject matter to all of life.

To know life is to know how to live it. Those who are wise gain in understanding old relationships better, this is their way of life. They gain in insight by building a new comprehensive relationship with life. This improves intuition, and cultivates awareness. Living with awareness and gaining by keeping an open mind is the reason why they attain a vision that comprehends a deeper meaning to life. With a holistic approach to life, they transcend their own ego self, and find serenity, and peace of mind. Aging becomes a beneficial process of savoring life.

Wisdom comes from living experiences, based upon a positive value system. You see what you should with the values you have given yourself.

Look deeper, see with insight, be objective, even minded, and the mind/body will be receptive thus increasing body power.

NEGATIVE VALUES AND INSIGHT

Incorrect judgment (delusion) predominates in those whom greed, envy, and egotism are strong. Negative values create agitation and anxiety which lead to false interpretation of situations. Greed hostility and malice initiate a state of mind that does not comply with the realities of the environment. Blame, anger, resentment cause a mental activity that uncontrollably fluctuate.

When the frame of reference is based upon a negative view of the world, external events are then experienced in a negative way. Revenge, envy, and jealousy keep the mind frustrated, anxious and disturbed. This uneasy mind sees falsely.

Emotionally we feel that which we vision to be true. Negative values not only cloud the vision, but also ruin the health of the body. Those who see with anger are prone to ulcers and nervousness.

Inspirational qualities that comfort the well-being of our health, and help us keep a tranquil mind, are lost as the body becomes ridged and inflexible with negative values.

Insight is a health giving factor. Delusion is an unhealthy factor.

SELF IMAGE AND VALUES

The director of a play, sees the whole drama without getting trapped into any one part. He sees each player as part of the drama. He maintains his mental distance as he views all the actors with objectivity. If a member of the cast is gone, the director can play any part. Or become involved with an entirely new play, with different costumes, and characters. Life is like the play, we play a part and think that we are really living to the fullest extent. While all the time we are asleep within the egos illusion of reality.

Shakespeare wrote:
    All the world's a stage
And all the men and women merely
    players,
They have their exits and their en-
    trances;
And one man in his time plays many
    parts,

Positive values eliminate the act, one transends the self, the ego image, and moves toward a holistic approach to life. the mind is then free to investigate the wonders of life. The Universe is diversified fathomable, a self image, an ego, a title, a culture, tradition, is only a small limited part of reality.

Justice, health, self esteem and joy flourish in abundance when we infuse our self with the vastness of the Universe. This fusion takes place with an open mind and with positive values.

MANAGEMENT, LEADERSHIP AND VALUES

Money, power, position and rank, do not make an individual effective in life or in management. Values produce effectiveness. Insight determines success in management.

Leadership administered by ego gratification gains no permanent advantage. High rank becomes a slave to its own oppressions, and aggressions. Rank, position, and cleverness do not save those in power who take self respect, and dignity away from others. Richness of maturity, psychological vitality, becomes impared when compassion and discretion are ignored.

Those who are in power - teachers, managers, foremen, parents, etc. - can increase their material goals by adding the humane dimension of personal development to their ways of leadership. Positive values make organizations and businesses effective, because constructive values produce good judgment, trust, and integrity, then there is respect and hospitality which generate enthusiasm, loyalty and a spirit of oneness.

Wise leaders share their power, they lead by following, their policy is to listen, support, and serve. Effective management takes pleasure in making others confident, and allowing everyone to be involved with decision-making policies. Lead by elevating the finer qualities of others, and you work as a team in harmony and unity.

Life is continuous. The way of leadership at work is extended to the family and friends. If you devaluate in your leadership you devaluate your life. You become the follower of your own leadership.

By focusing on humane concepts, common day activities are transferred into enriching experiences. A deeper bond strengthens relationships. The next transaction takes place on a higher level of consciousness.

Each individual is a new thinking pattern, an adventure in difference. Innumerable possibilities are possible in any social interaction. Through relationships you rediscover that which you already know. Those who are wisere-learn the same thing many times. This is the art of living. Watch how values work, be free to mold and reshape your own thinking. Everyone has something to offer you. Each of us is a teacher.

When the label of leader is placed in your hands use it to inspire and to cultivate trust and harmony. Give care and attention to people and they will heighten and intensify their talents.

VALUES, REALITY AND SOCIETY

Life is revealed when faith in positive values are used to build your character traits. By putting your trust in that which is positive you have put your trust in the powers of nature. The full powers of the mind and body will be experienced. The seed of fortune will grow, you will be rewarded for your thoughts and actions. Your mind will be tranquil even under stressful situations. You will have a sense of equality for all people, ages, sexes, and races. You will be open to new information from whatever source it comes from. You will respond with clarity, and alertness. Perception is accurate, so body movements are quick and accurate. You will keep in touch with the totality of each situation. A deep sense of self-trust, personal integrity grows, along with compassion for others. Life becomes an adventure that promotes good will. Because you are really living, the fear of death is gone, so is resentment and anger.

Values chosen create your reality

Reality is the values you use

Each moment is a reflection of your reality

You always lay your path before you in the
form of thoughts

Being positive, cultivating faith in benevolence,
balances the internal body, and
strengthens the mental powers

You then become connected with nature with your
own nature

You are the Universe, a part of nature, reflecting
back on itself

The balance of justice is found in understanding our own capabilities. Humans are victory oriented. If they are taught the skills to handle life, to understand how values work then they will win. The primary duty of society is to help people raise the level of their own humanity. This is the only security, the best insurance. We are fully civilized when human problems are solved by people working in harmony, cooperating, and communicating at a level that inspires each and all.

What are values? They are the fabric of society. The base of all interaction. The clay that molds destiny. With constructive values, the comprehension of life takes place on a higher level, where the development of character is advanced, where the deeper insights into nature are observed, followed and encouraged. Stress, nervousness, depression envy, greed, negative identity images, should be minor occurances, not common everyday problems.

Human potential should never go undeveloped. Never should an individual be sacrificed for lack of self knowledge. By magic we expect people to understand life. Why risk life to fate or luck? Why should children have to figure out life on their own? Taking the risk that they might really believe that negative belief systems work and put their trust in nonproductive, self defeating thoughts.

Teach the mind and body relationship. Show how positive values improve body power and mental stability.

Enrichment programs should be the major part of every school program. Psychological growth must keep pace with material growth. Reading, writing, and arithmetic are tools to be used to function better in the mechanical world. They do not guarantee humane principles or common sense. The important underlying factors behind all deeds, are the mental states. Values are the tools that open up the door to higher education. Education without a value system is hazardous.

Drug abuse and crime, are problems that could be greatly reduced with self improvement programs. Conditions are created by what we avoid. Trillions of dollars have been spent in armament, how much for human development? Neglect equals defect. The rules of cause and effect apply to all of life.

Natural laws maintain their own credibility. People often think that good virtues, ethics, and positive values, are old fashioned, out of date, unworkable. Ethics, and values are not old fashioned, or new fashioned, they are just a part of human nature. They operate for or against you at every moment. They are unavoidable.

Ethics are laughed at, philosophy is viewd as a study for intellectuals. This type of thinking is a result of not being aware of life. You cannot avoid making decisions, forming attitudes, and reshaping your self image. By your own nature you are a philosopher. You spend most of the time talking to yourself, thinking, sharing ideas and deciding on what to do.

The more you understand life, the more you open up to your own philosophical awareness. With the increase of awareness, you will soon realize that ethics are fun. That positive values are the greatest of highs. Life based on positive values is thrilling.

Social justice also demands personal integrity based upon a strong philosophical balance.

World peace isn't secured by bylaws, rules, and amendments. This is only a temporary peace. Permanent peace is secured by an internal understanding in relationship to what we are, and raising the level of consciousness.

The Human Equation
Values   x   Belief System   =   Quality of Life

Part II

BELIEF SYSTEM

Everyone is special, but nobody is the exception. We are members of the Universe, a part of a human dilemna, living together on an island in space. Unfortunately we have used race, nation, and other differences to build artificial barriers throughout the brotherhood of man.

Antiproductive habits, attitudes and identity labels are naturally developed throughout life. Harmful ideas, and images, curtail the human potential.

If you take a classroom of third or fourth graders and ask them to put the winners on one side of the room, and the losers on the other side, they can do this easily. At a young age, stigmas, identities, of winners and loser are already being established. The theory of good and bad is used to determine personal worth. Young children without a mature mind select identities, then values are chosen to fit the identity.

If you were to ask a high school student which school is the best one, he would say that his alma mater was superior. If he were to transfer to another school, how long would it take until he thought the new school was superior? Probably two or three months. Innocently, we chose what we have, where we are, be it location, city, state, club, culture, and take a critical view of that to which we do not belong.

At birth we are born innocent, without an opinion, view of the world or attitude, the basic instincts alone dominate. At the age of two or three, part of the instincts emerge and form a new unique

17

power. This new power will declare its independence, and proceed to constantly evaluate, change, and remold ideas and concepts, of what is useful, real, and necessary. An ego is born.

The unavoidable mental journey through life has started. The mind will change its views of life because of experiences and information, but during its growth, behavior traits and beliefs become firm and solidified. The mind builds its own unique belief system.

A child is born helpless; his mind is receptive to the environment, and is easily patterned and influenced. Before the child has a chance to analyze or think for himself, he is already molded. His values and ways of behavior are established. Through childhood various roles are prescribed by society. One is expected to have a strong ego, a solid image, to forge ahead, and manipulate the world. Self interest and egotism marks the way of life.

We live for a time immersed in life unconsciously aware of ourselves. At brief intervals we may contemplate upon what we are from where we have passed. Our belief system of the past will reinforce itself. All of life will reinforce the belief that we have. We will see what we believe to be true. Within our special picture of the world, is a reality that is a perfect truth mixed with illusion.

We are metamorphosized into many things, divided and subtracted from as the changing personal views of the world change, emerge and disappear.

Personal growth happens when old views and ideas mix with new ones. This is how individuals and cultures change. Society seems powerful, and secure, somebody reveals a new secret of nature, a new door is opened. Instead of eagerly accepting the new concept, it is usually rejected, because of the cultural belief system. New discoveries are at first overpowered by old world beliefs.

Philosophers, and inventors like Galileo, Roger Bacon, and Socrates, were humiliated and scorned. Why? Because people don't realize that their belief system is only a small part of reality.

When presented with a new idea, the last thing people do is to question their own belief system, and this should be the first thing that they do.

Life might be compared to viewing a puzzle that is partly together, it's full of isolated parts. The picture is not clear it remains mysterious and illusive. The puzzle can be put together in a form that shows harmony, unity and continuity. But this unity is beyond words, and concrete ideas, it is intuitive and poetic. The major purpose of life, the fun of living, is to put the puzzle of life together better and understand the logical, and intuitive aspects of nature.

The major goal
in life
is to develop
your greatest potential

THE INVISIBLE AND THE BELIEF SYSTEM

There is no deviation from the invisible. From the invisible all things appear. The invisible always manifests itself first, before the visible is seen.

The invisible laws of nature integrate with the organic and inorganic.

To fully comprehend the nature of things, the forces of the invisible should be considered with great care.

The invisible forces are among all human actions. Lives are altered when the invisible is altered.

Cultures grow and disappear, peace is declared, then, war. The power behind growth and distruction first declares itself in the invisible form.

Ideas, concepts, will to power and anger, are generated from within, then projected externally.

Listed are some of the invisible aspects of human nature; inspiration, faith, hope, courage, empathy, thoughts, sympathy, love, fear, willpower, perseverance, attitude, opportunity, plans, worry, greed, values, envy, jealousy, modesty, humility, discretion, kindness, arrogance, power of influence, anger, anxiety, egotism, and spirit.

These are just some of the invisible forces, that are used to form cultures, belief systems, group structures and inner reactions.

As humans, we use the invisible to form reality, because we are the creators of words, thoughts, and ideas. Within the realm of creativity exists unlimited mental concept possibilities, that can be combined to create endless belief systems, cultures and ways of life.

Thought impressions are the blueprints that we use to develop our view of the world. What we are now is a result of what we have thought. When thoughts are reshaped, so is the belief system; circumstances are then changed, the future altered. We live our lives through the thoughts we accept and use. Any thought given consideration and held over a period of time manifests itself into the belief system.

Examine past history, each period of time has its own unique way of life. The 20's, 40's and 60's all had different trends, fads, beliefs, all represent a temporary cultural agreement, a way of being, a psychological environment that was molded from the invisible. Each period of time, has its own myth, its own idea of what is real. Each society, each decade creates its own way of dress, belief system, way of thought. From the invisible we become what we are.

THE SUBCONSCIOUS MIND
AND
THE BELIEF SYSTEM

Life is an art to be lived. Each moment is an intuitional experience, a feeling, that flows beyond the limits of logic. Experiences are transformed into feelings, these feelings are forever remembered by the subconscious mind.

Close your eyes, do you feel the same way here as you do someplace else? Do you feel the same way at home as you do at work? Choose several locations, you will notice that you actually feel different in any given room, house, or town. Groups of people have their special feel. Art music, symbols, ceremonies, dances, spontaneously arouse a variety of different feelings.

A witch doctor helps his patients to heal by chanting, dancing, and the use of ceremonies. He can also kill by placing a spell upon someone. The effect of the spell is so powerful that the victim dies within a few days.

In a modern culture the patient goes through a ceremony of going to a doctor for cure. The doctor then gives the patient the permission to heal by giving him instructions and a placebo pill.

The placebo pill is milk sugar, it has no healing properities. With faith, the patient's disease is cured. The placebo pill effect isn't just a general reaction of feeling better. Specific body reactions take place depending upon what the doctor says, and how the patient is willing to accept the information. Even side effects occur, depending upon the belief of what should happen.

The language of the body is visulization. Through visulization blood can be sent to the feet and hands, making them warm. Body temperature can be changed at will, heart rate lowered, blood sugar level changed, hypertension controlled, respiration and pulse rate lowered.

It has been suggested that about 70 to 80 percent of disease is caused by the mind (psychosomatic). If a disease is caused with the mind it can often be reversed with the mind. By changing your belief system you change your health. Anxiety, nervousness, ulcers, and headaches, are common health problems that are caused by negative visulization.

Anger and resentment, keep the body in a state of hyper activity, this is unnatural and unhealthful. As you acquire thoughts that promote positive values, you become calmer, and healthier.

Biofeedback, machines have been used by cancer patients with great success.

The cancer patients learn how to relax and use visulization to destroy the cancer cells. They alter the disease by changing their belief system. They learn how to live and deal with stress in a relaxed calm way.

Health is a state of consciousness, healing improves, when the state of consciousness is elevated.

We cannot change stress or problems, they will always exist. Since we can't change these problems and eliminate them, we must change our thoughts, and reverse our negative interpretations. Stress is linked with many body ailments, cancer has just been added to the list.

You must face life, problems, and make decisions, there is no escape. Choose to build your belief system with positive values the life you save will be yours.

Part III

SUMMARY

Values   x   Belief System   =   Your Quality Of Life

VALUES

POSITIVE VALUES	NEGATIVE VALUES
Equanimity	Envy
Modesty	Greed
Respect	Jealousy
Kindness	Egotism
Empathy	Hatred
Admiration	Arrogance
Sympathy	Revenge
Quality of life with	Quality of life with
Positive Values	Negative Values
Adaptability	Inharmonious
Confident	Nervousness
Rapture	Agitation
Proficiency	Perplexity
Perceptive	False view
Supportive	Oppressive
Psychological endurance	Worry
Mind and Body unity	Mind and Body divided
Body energy remains stable	Body energy raises
Unconditional friendship	Resentments, wants revenge
Self control	Lose of emotional control
Considers all facts	Prejudice
Honest	Secretive, clever
Good leader	Poor leader

Values are formed. This form is called character. Through this value form called character we see, and feel.

1. We develop our sight with values
   Positive values = Clarity of vision
   Negative values = False interpretations

2. Values = Experiences
   The world is a reflection of our value system.

3. Values = Quality of emotions.

4. Values = The level of body power, balance and co - ordination.

Values x Belief System = Your Quality Of Life

BELIEF SYSTEM

By virtue of our own nature we combine ideas and concepts, to create a belief system, this is our truth. Whatever our belief system is, we live it, see it, feel it, and tell others about it.

As people combine their personal beliefs, a custom or tradition is born. Group beliefs are so powerful that the individual will is often over powered. People get caught up in the psychological environment of the culture. They stop thinking for themselves, roles are established, people no longer are unique characters but imitators.

People forget that life belongs to them, they deserve the freedom to create their own uniqueness. Life belongs to those who enhance their own potential, expand their capabilities, and build their way of life separate from all others.

Structured society is very valuable. People need a foundation, to establish a compromise, so they may live together in harmony. But we lose an important aspect of our life when we neglect our own abilities to stay open minded and continuously flourish.

The nature of belief systems

1.   Belief systems keep you from receiving new and valuable information.

2.   Belief systems reinforce themselves. If we view life from just one perspective, and other people reinforce our views, and we reinforce theirs, then everyone of us gets stuck in a belief system and close off our minds. Life becomes limited. The diversity of the Universe is ignored. Life is turned over to group agreement, rather than self investigation.

3.   Positive values can be used by a group belief system to produce negative results. How many people throughout history have been killed and tortured in the name of justice and love?

*Watch out for your
belief system
it can keep you from
receiving good information*

Values   x   Belief System   =   Your Quality Of Life
QUALITY OF LIFE

Quality of life manifests itself in all things that you do.
1. The way you experience your daily life.
2. Mental and physical health.
3. Body strength
4. Insight, wisdom, perception
5. Integrity
6. Character
7. Social relationships
8. Reactions, alertness
9. Patience, mental calm
10. Intuition
11. Level of harmony
12. Tolerance
13. Psychological endurance.
14. The spirit to do, to be, to want, to know, to think.

Since you have to play
the game of Life
anyway,
why not learn
how to win

THE HUMAN EQUATION
AND HOW TO ANALYZE IT

Nature is represented in polar opposites
Some of these basic polar opposites are:

Man	Women
Light	Darkness
Action	Reaction
Energy	Matter
Wave	Particle
Positive	Negative
Centrifugal	Centripetal

Polar opposites found in human nature are:

Left cerebral hemisphere characteristics	Right cerebral hemisphere characteristics
Logic	Intuitive
Anal/tic	Creative
Verbal	Feeling
Linear	Poetic

This part of our human nature seeks to be analytical.

This part of our human nature is intuitive.

This polarity chooses values and belief systems.

This polarity knows that life is a quality to be experienced.

This logical part of our nature should view the human equation with a philosophical attitude, and use it to design a better life, for ourselves and everyone else.

This poetic part of our nature should view the human equation as a work of art, a quality of ourselves, beyond words.

The greatest artist lives creatively

He knows that life is an art. to be experienced

A mystery to be lived, that goes beyond the limits of the ego

Part IV

PHYSICAL TESTS

MIND/BODY RELATIONSHIP
HOW TO BRING THEM INTO HARMONY
INCREASING PHYSICAL STRENGTH AND
MENTAL STABILITY
THE ULTIMATE WAY TO STOP STRESS, ANXIETY
AND IMPROVE ATHLETIC ABILITY

This portion of the book will show you how values, thoughts, and focus of attention, can weaken and strengthen the body. You will learn how to deal with stress, anxiety, and emergency situations.

Everyone can learn how to deal with every aspect of their life in a more effective and efficient way. Step by step you will learn how to become more in harmony with your own natural strengths. You will see how thoughts change body power. Enrichment of your life will come from exploring this way of balancing the mind and body.

The main concept is to give you a new perspective about your own abilities. To prove the power of positive values, and improve your efficiency in everything that you do.

The information presented here cannot be avoided. You are involved with all of these exercise concepts all the time. The importance of the following chapters is to become aware of what you are already doing, and use your own natural abilities more effectively.

You are constantly projecting your attention into objects, events, and people. When you change your focus of attention, you automatically alter your body power, balance, stability, coordination, and mental state.

The body easily follows the direction of focus. The further the distance that you focus your attention, the weaker your body stability becomes.

If you direct your focus toward the hips, you will be powerful, move with natural balance and harmony. The power of the body is located in the pelvic area. When you take advantage of this natural balance area, the power from the hips will be used when you perform physical tasks. You take on the characteristics of a natural athlete. You operate in a holistic manner, with total control of body and mind.

The body and mind relationship is one of the most important aspects to understand, because its the knowledge of this relationship that can give you control over stress, anxiety, and improve your athletic ability.

First we will examine the physical process of what happens when you focus your attention on external objects.

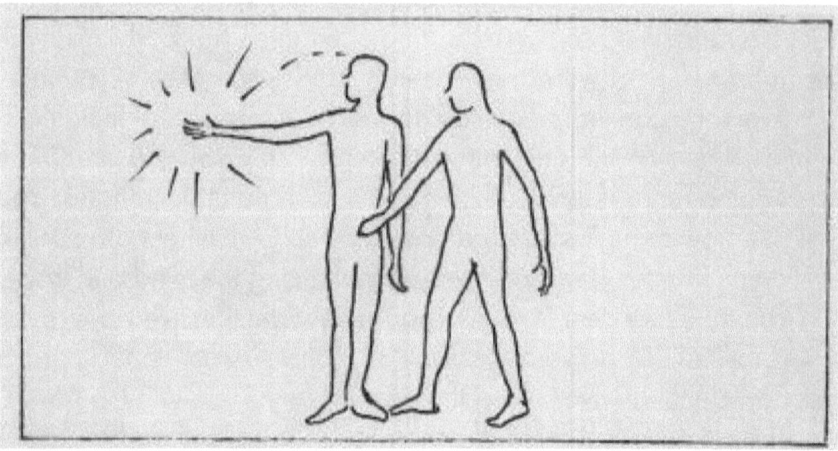

FIGURE 1

Beginning position, A has the right arm extended and will be tested for body power. B, will be pushing on the hip.

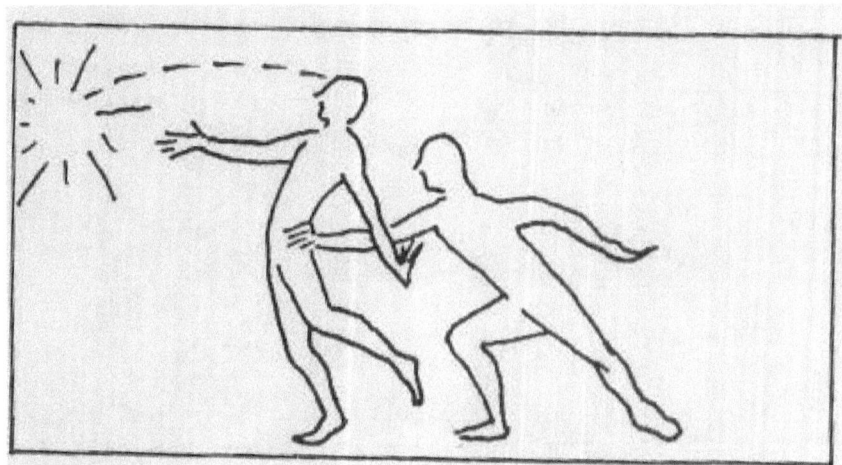

FIGURE 2

A, concentrates on the right hand. Then partner B, applys pressure in the direction of A's focus of attention. B, will notice that very little pressure is needed to push A off balance.

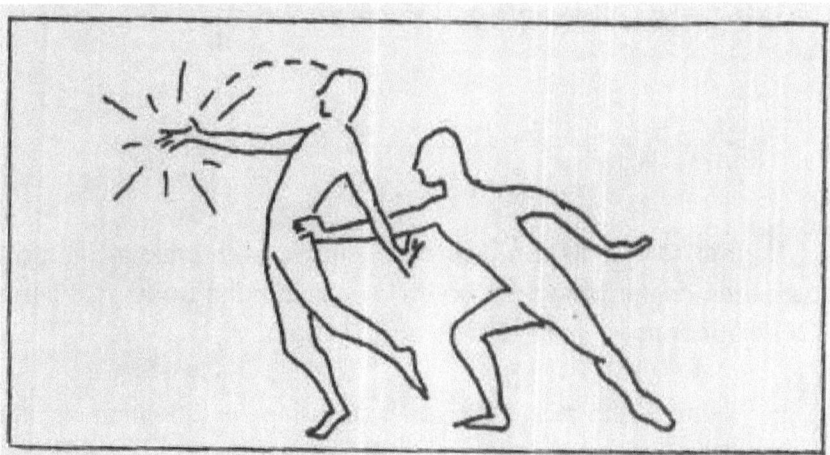

FIGURE 3

A's concentration is focused on the wall, or out a window. B, applys pressure in the direction of A's focus of attention. The amount of pressure required to move A off balance, will be much less than in figure 2, because the focus was further away from the body.

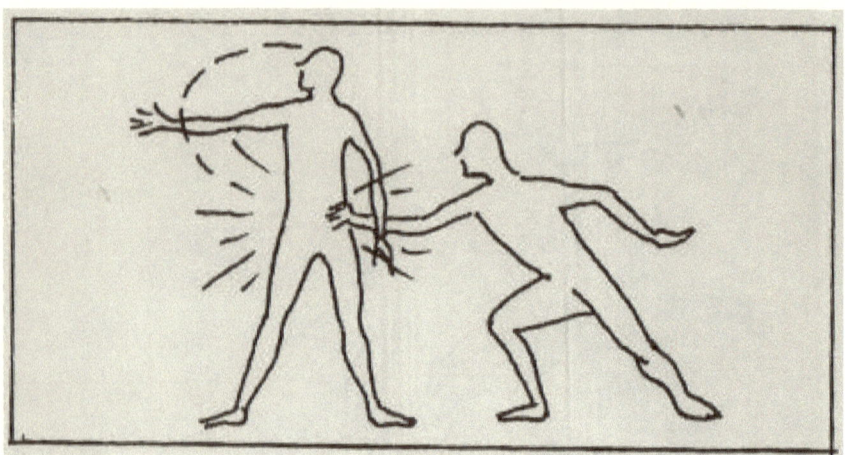

FIGURE 4

A, focuses attention on the hips. B applies pressure. A will notice that the body power has more than doubled.

As illustrated in Figures, 1-4, the focus of attention was directly related to physical strength and stability.

The next example can best be illustrated with athletes. In most cases their center of focus is so far away from the body, that there is a tremendous loss of balance and strength.

In Figure 5, the tennis player is focusing his attention on the end of the racket, as B pushes, the balance is easily lost. In Figure 6, A, is focusing on the hips, and as B pushes there isn't any lose of balance.

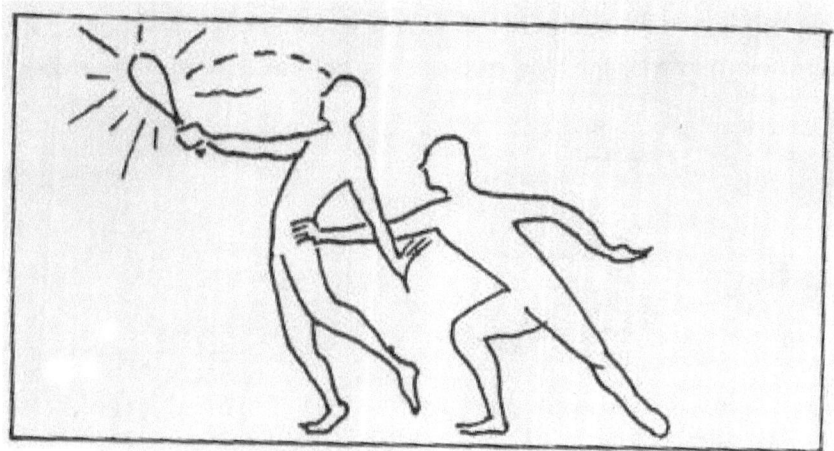

FIGURE 5

In tennis, concentration is on the racket. Balance is lost because of this outward projection. Body movement is not smooth, changing directions with the feet will be awkward.

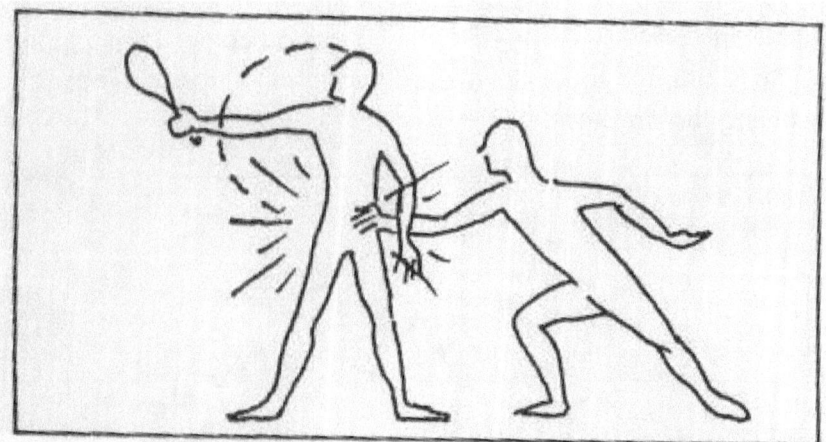

FIGURE 6

As in Figure 4, bring the concentration back into the hips. Now the tennis player will be fast, and natural in movement, along with total body harmony.

In Figure 7, the golfer is focusing his attention on the ball or end of the club, as B pushes the hips, A's balance is lost. If B were to pull the club he would also easily off balance A. In Figure 8, A is focusing downward toward the hips, as B pushes, he realizes that A is powerful.

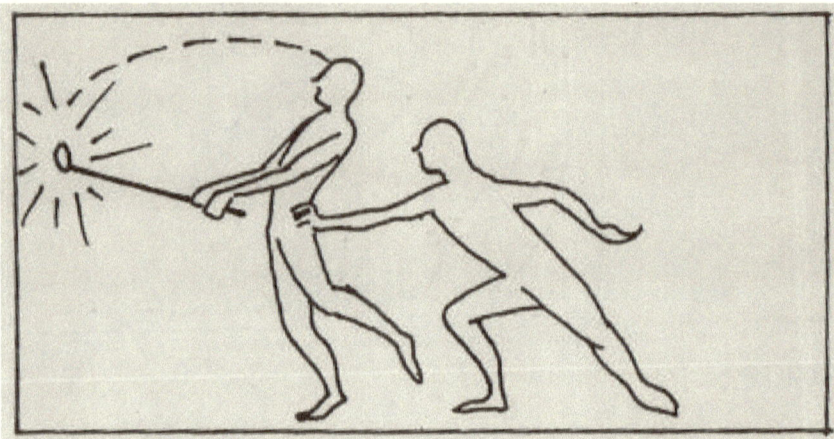

FIGURE 7

In golf, if the total focus is on the ball, or end of the club the center of balance will be there also. Harmony of motion is lost, along with hitting power. Power, and unity of action comes from the hips. You must learn to focus downward through the hips and legs, also including the arms and club.

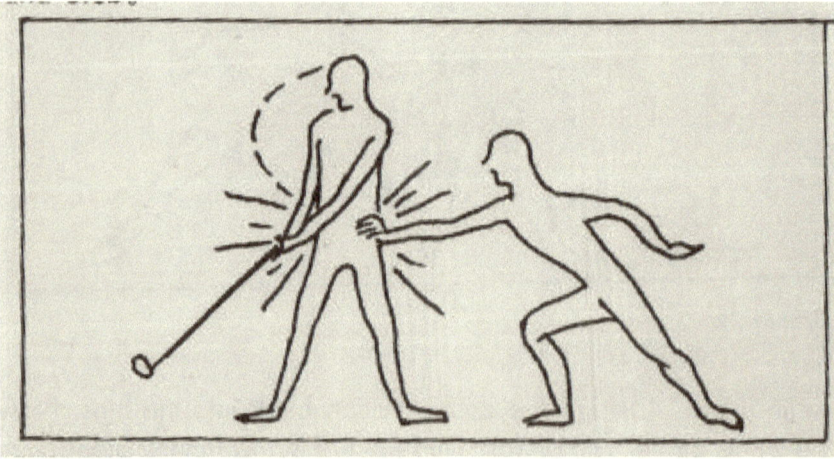

FIGURE 8, Focus is on hip.

FIGURE 9

Focus on the end of a bat, and have partner B, push you from the hips or pull on the bat.

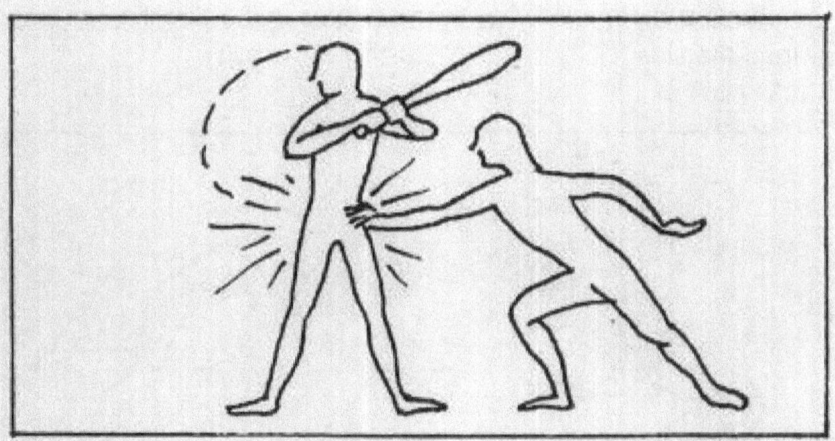

FIGURE 10

Focus is on hips, baseball player is powerful with his swing.

FIGURE 11

Football players focus on other players, and are easily tackled. This test can be done with three people. Have someone stand in front of you, then focus your attention toward him, as in figure 3 and 11. Then have someone slowly push your hips in the direction of focus or from the side.

FIGURE 12

Test the body position this time by pushing in the direction of focus and from the sides. You will notice that when the hips are focused upon, there is stability in every direction.

As demonstrated in the previous examples, athletes center their focus so far away from the body, that there is a tremendous loss of balance, and body power. In tennis, golf, and baseball, the players usually project their attention toward the end of the racket, bat, or golf club. By doing this they have lost the power of the hips, coordination, timing, and balance is awkward.

A football player gives up his running and tackling power by focusing on the other players. When the players throw a pass or receive the football, there is an urge to focus on the football.

When a javelin thrower prepares to throw, his concentration is usually on his hand where he holds the javelin. He loses the power he needs because his focus is upward on the hand and away from the hip.

Weight lifters get themselves psyched up to lift enormous weights. They need the power of the entire body, especially the hips and legs. Their concentration usually shoots down the arm and into the weights that they are lifting. The lift becomes ineffective, mind and body are not in unity.

In all of these situations the athlete focused their attention on the object or events. They gave up their own stability to an external situation.

The basic rule to follow, so that you maintain balance and strength, is to concentrate downward into the hips, instead of into the object or events that are taking place. Then you keep your power, and move as a total unit.

With team sports, the focus of attention is extended over long distances toward outward events, the body becomes extremely vulnerable. It is very important, especially with these contact sports, to keep the downward flow of concentration. The same rule applies to all sports. Bowlers should focus from the hips, not the ball. Gymnasts, dancers, divers, should use the hips as their center of balance.

In Figure 13, the high jumper may be relaxed and feel a sense of body unity, but as he approaches the cross bar, he has a tendency to focus on it, and before he jumps, the power of the hips is already gone.

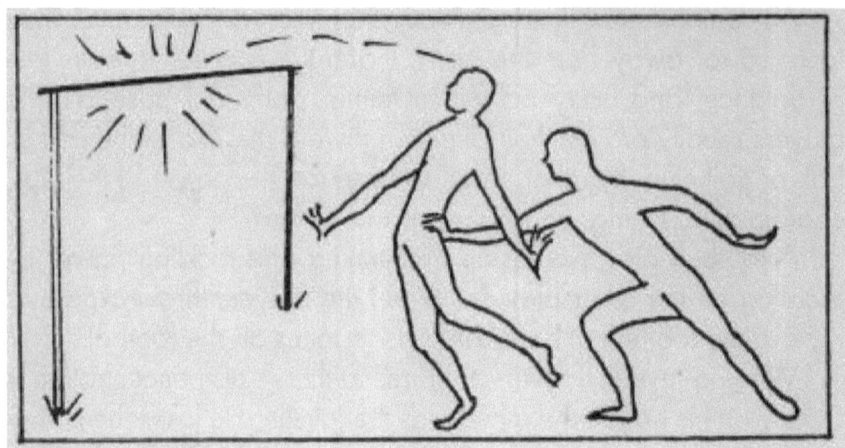

FIGURE 13

A high jumper projects his focus toward the cross bar, losing his power.

FIGURE 14.

Focus is downward.

LOSING MENTAL AND PHYSICAL STABILITY
IN VARIOUS SITUATIONS

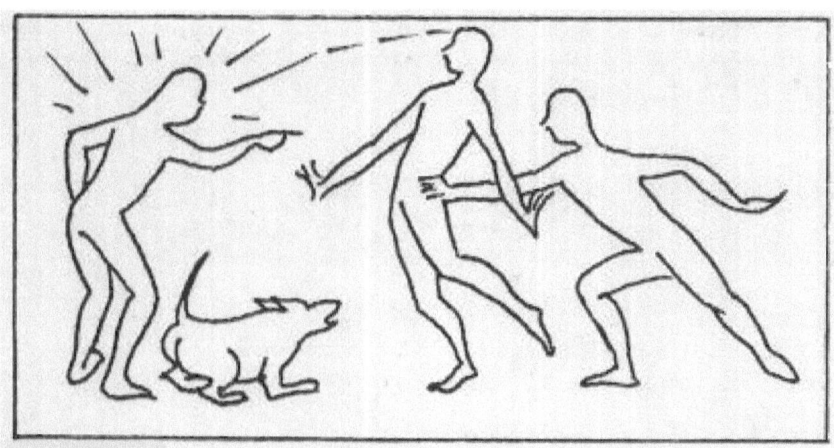

FIGURE 15

In stressful situations, there is a tendency to project your focus of attention toward other people or toward the problem.

Physical strength is lost in the same way as when concentration was focused on an object. In the case of a conflict you lose your emotional control as well as giving up physical power.
WHEN PHYSICAL FOCUS IS GIVEN UP TOWARD A PROBLEM, SO IS MENTAL STABILITY.

As you experience a threat, think of it as moving toward you, and THROUGH your body. Instead of rejecting it, accept it as a source of extra energy. Take this energy through the legs and into the ground.

With this concept in mind, stress, problems, threats, and anxieties, become sources of positive energy, that give you more vitality.

If your job is high pressured or stressful, you should relax, and prepare yourself to experience high energy every day.

These are some mental concepts that will unify the mind and body. They automatically give you mental control and physical strength.

In Figure 16, A sits in a chair and concentrates on the hips and legs. B, slowly applies pressure under the chin as he pushes backwards. A is very strong.

In Figure 17, A focuses his attention on the wall behind him. When B pushes under the chin, A is very weak.

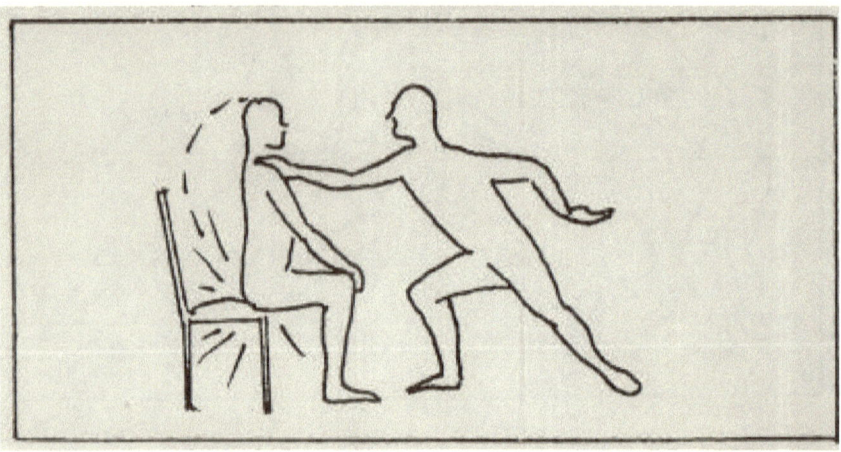

FIGURE 16

A focuses on the hip, chair, and floor. B pushes slowly under the chin. A's balance is very powerful.

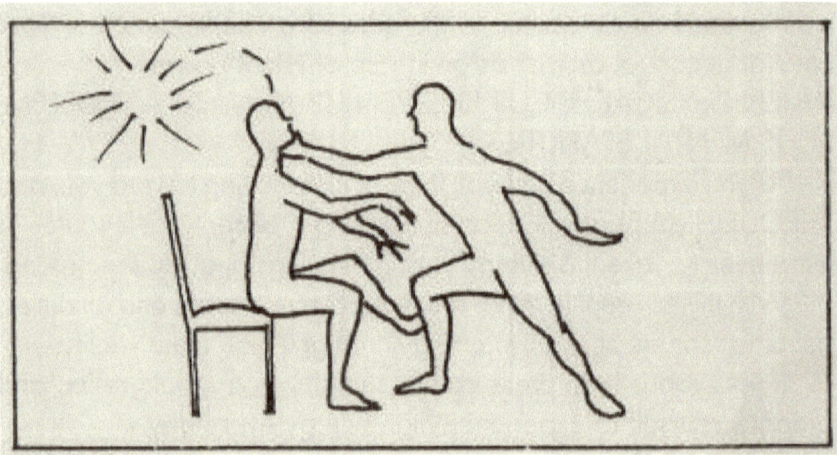

FIGURE 17

A focuses his concentration on an object behind him, but faces forward. B, pushes under the chin. A moves backwards with ease.

Figure 18, is an example of how this exercise might apply to an emergency situation.

By focusing on a vehicle too close behind you, there is a mind, body imbalance, which hinders reaction, perception and coordination. If a bicyclist suddenly turns in front of your car your response isn't immediate, the mind and body are not unified.

FIGURE 18

Driver is focused mentally on the car behind him, losing body coordination and reation time.

Firemen and policemen face crisis situations which require full efficiency. This efficiency is adversely affected if they misdirect their focus of attention. The policeman's attention would be grasped by a threat, gun, weapon, or words. The fireman by fire, ladders, people, and rescue operations.

There are many stress producing professions, where the employees are overwhelmed with problems, pressures, frustrations, schedules, work problems, etc. The working environment can be a powerful force that takes the focus of attention from the employee, causing nervousness, job burn out, anxiety, strain, tension and lack of concentration.

In figures 19, 20, and 21, you can see how a policeman directs his focus of attention on his baton, handcuffs, or gun. There is also the possibility that his attention will be focused on the suspect. In any case an imbalance is created and the policeman is at a physical disadvantage when his concentration is diverted outwardly, instead of inwardly.

FIGURE 19

Policeman focuses on his baton

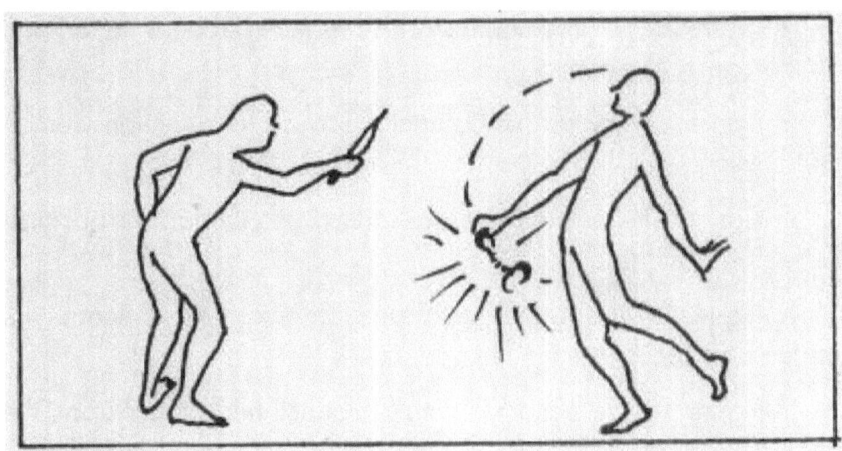

FIGURE 20

Policeman focuses on his handcuffs

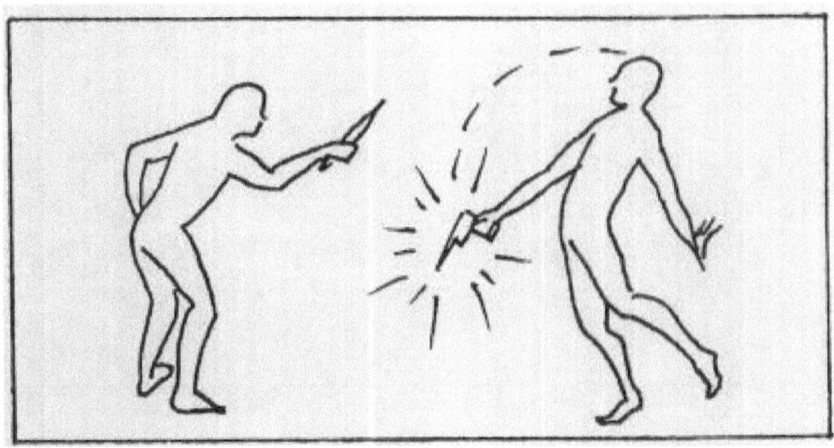

FIGURE 21

Policeman focuses on his gun

In Figure 22, the fireman loses his balance because he focused on the end of the axe.

In Figure 23, he lost his balance because his attention was on the air pack.

In Figure 24, he loses leverage and drops the ladder because he focused on the end of it.

In Figure 25, he loses mental and physical unity, because he projects his focus into the fire.

In Figure 26, he becomes weak because he focused upon the one who he was helping.

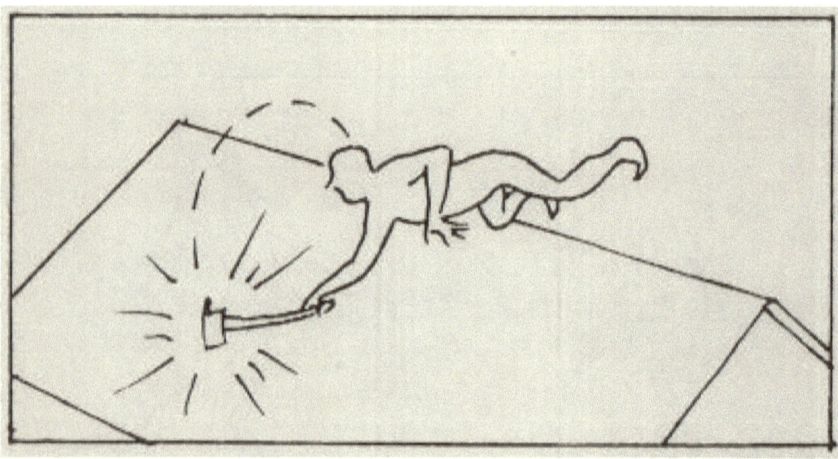

FIGURE 22

Fireman focuses on end of axe and loses balance.

FIGURE 23

By focusing on air tank the fireman slips or falls easily.

FIGURE 24

Fireman loses control of ladder because his focus is on the top of the ladder.

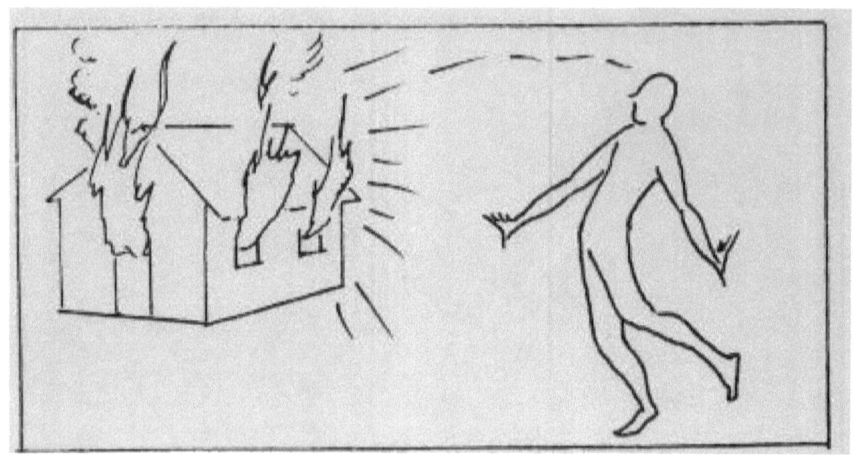

FIGURE 25

Fire and excitement take the focus of attention

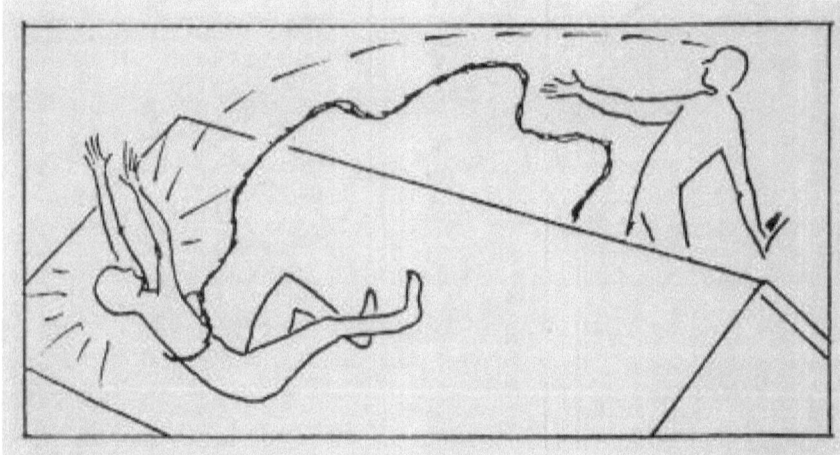

FIGURE 26

Someone in need of help can take away body power

FIGURE 27

In Figure 27, you can see how the qualitative aspect of your mind can determine your balance. Play some music and whether you like it or not, pretend that you don't like it, reject it mentally, hold it away from you, shield it, block it out. As illustrated in figure 27, have partner B, grasp your chin and pull you backwards. You will notice that the amount of strength required to pull you off balance was very little.

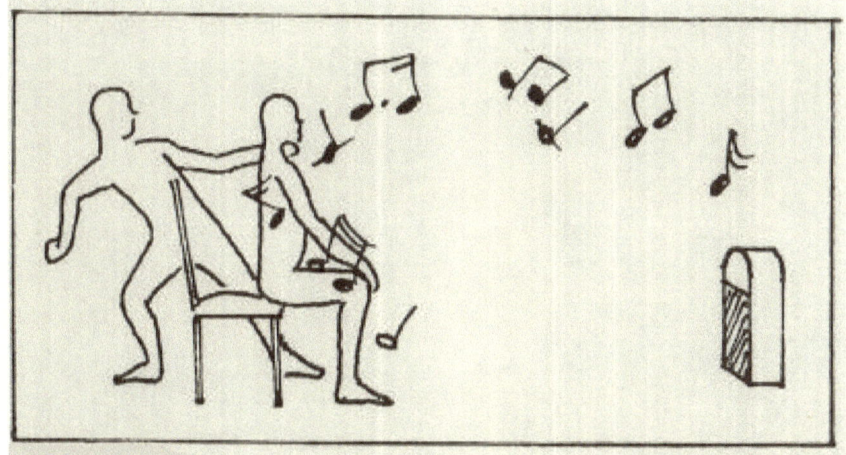

FIGURE 28

Let the music flow through you and enjoy it. Now have B, pull back on your chin. You will now notice that you are strong.

FOCUS OF ATTENTION

Focus of attention goes on continuously in common daily activities such as: playing a piano, washing dishes, eating, having a conversation, playing cards, picking up a hammer, etc. You are always changing your focus, and when you do the mind and body relationship changes.

The suitable condition is when the focus is downward, because the mental faculties are calm, tranquil and under control, the physical powers are also at their optimal level.

This mental physical unity is how deep concentration is acquired, along with emotional stability, and physical strength.

The process of acquiring the attitude and feelings of acceptance, and choosing to focus downward, doesn't mean that you are avoiding the situaion, it means that you are giving more of yourself in a controllable effective vital way. Actually you are projecting, but in a downward way.

Value of Thoughts

POSITIVE VALUES AND FOCUS OF ATTENTION

THE MIND AND BODY ARE IN UNITY, AND
MAXIMUM BODY POWER IS IN THE HIPS, WHEN
POSITIVE VALUES, AND ATTITUDES PREVAIL

POSITIVE THOUGHTS CULTIVATE A HIGH QUALITY
MENTAL STATE, THAT KEEPS THE BODY AND MIND
RELAXED, CALM, POISED, AND POWERFUL

THIS IS WHY YOU GAIN OR LOSE BODY POWER,
ALONG WITH EMOTIONAL STABILITY,
DEPENDING UPON YOUR VALUE SYSTEM

In Figures 29 and 30, you will learn that values equal your quality of body strength.

FIGURE 29

Think of a situation where you were angry or irritated, now have partner B, pull you forward. Negative values weaken the center of balance.

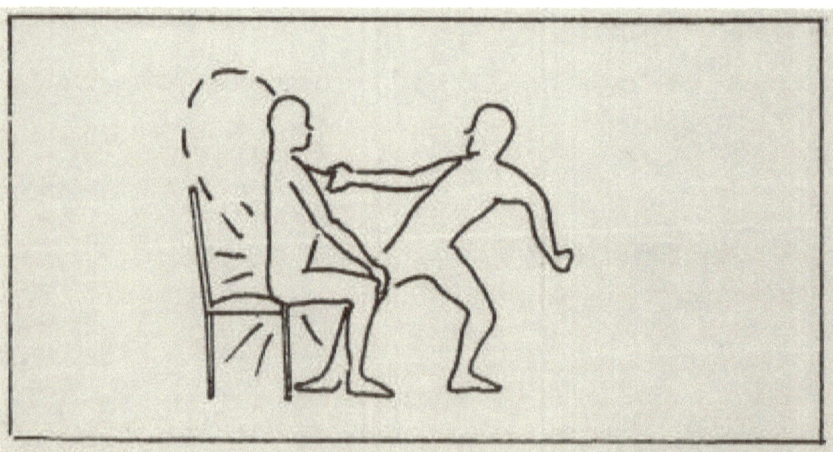

FIGURE 30

Think of a situation where you were helpful and sought only to improve the conditions by being kind and hospitable. By this way of thought, you have trippled your body power. Test, by having partner B, pull you forward. Positive values strengthen the body and calms the mind.

Learn to accept all things with the eyes and ears, relax do not resist or reject. Keep the idea that a flow of energy is moving downward, and that any external noise or threat will add to this strength.

Comprehension of this concept will eliminate stress, and anxiety. Become the quality of strength as in figure 30.

ELIMINATING STRESS, ANXIETY, AND PROBLEMS

When the environment is stressful there is generally a rush of excitement, energy, and blood toward the head or legs depending upon how the situation is perceived. Embalance or balance is determined by the interpretation of a situation.

Negative values cause anxiety, anger, and tension, which causes the body energy to flow upward.

Positive values allow the mind and body to work under stress with control and harmony. Mental activity remains calm and alert, while the body stays relaxed and flexible. Emotions and tension are not held in the muscles, it flows downward through the body. The stress energy is wisely used as vitality, rather than in the form of agitation or anger.

Attitudes and values are the basic building blocks to your better future, the way to stop nervousness, anxiety, worry and gain evenmindness, insight and body power. As you steadily acquire more positive values, and elevate the qualities of empathy, admiration and respect, the mental state deepens and strengthens. There is a new sense of energy (rapture). This quality of energy neutralizes stressful situations. With this quality of life you save your self from the daily problems that can irritate you if you are in a lower mental state.

Think back to the times when you have been in a room where a coworker was depressed and before the day was over you were some what down. You focused upon their depression, you let them own your feelings. Consider your last stressful situation, where after it was all over you arrived home with your neck muscles tense and tight. You focused your attention into the problem, probably using a negative attitude, your body energy raised from the hips and centered in the back of your neck. You held tension there. If you get mad, irritated, the focus is naturally upward.

By understanding how values change the energy, and focus of attention, you will realize the importance of programming a positive value system for yourself. You will be aware of what you can do to build confidence, body power, and work effectively on the job while you are under stress.

If the environment is negative and threatening, you must realize that it is up to you to interprete the situation in a positive way. Think of a problem, or pressure, as giving you more vitality, more energy. With this extra energy you are able to do more, exercise better, run longer, read more books, give more to your job performance. With this positive approach you maintain control of your mental and physical qualities. Heart rate and blood pressure are lowered, muscles stay relaxed, digestion is better.

Your values equal your quality of life.

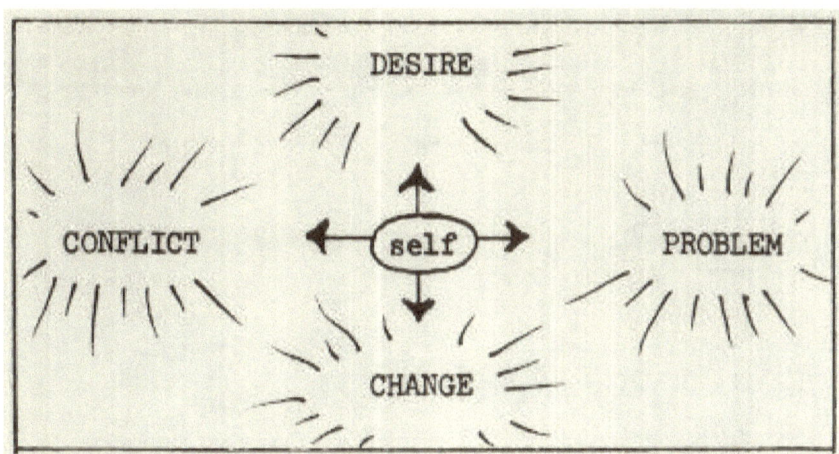

FIGURE 31

In figure 31, the self is represented as being small, because change, problems, conflict and desire have been focused upon. Body balance and emotional control has been given up to some other object, person, or event.

DESIRE The more you want something, the more it owns you. The mind never stops wanting. Many people give themselves up to desires.

PROBLEMS Problems will always be a part of life, but they are just a part of it. Interpret problems in a positive way, don't focus into them, let the problem be a small part of your total life. Feel as though the problem is flowing through you, giving your life more vitality and experience.

CHANGE Change is the way of nature. If you reject or dislike change then you are in trouble. Look forward to change, learn to enjoy it, expect it, blend with it.

CONFLICT Its the ego, the self image, the mental story you have that causes most of your conflicts. Learn to keep a mental distance, observe. This way you will deal more objectively and accurately with the situation, and maintain your self control. Live with forgiveness, and unconditional love.

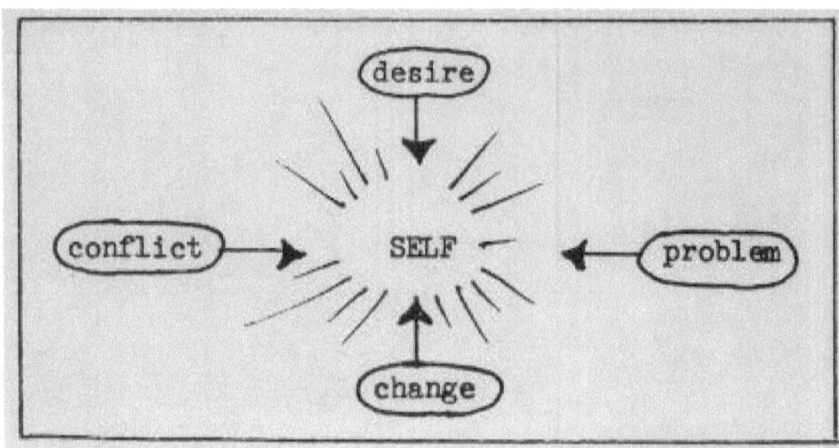

FIGURE 32

In figure 32, Desire, problems, change, and conflict, are seen as part of the Universe, the self is large, expanded observing with acceptance.

There is a sense of harmony, as the self openly, honestly, and respectively faces life.

The motto in figure 32 might be: Take pleasure in making others happy.

Part V

THINGS TO THINK ABOUT

Lets examine the word love, and see how this one word takes on new meaning as we reexperience it.

When we are very young our parents tell us, "we love you," which is usually accompanied with a hug. Our perception of love is based upon this experience. When we get a little older, about seven to ten years of age, love takes a new meaning because of our dog, playmates, and toys. Between the ages of sixteen and twenty-two, we find a new dimension of love, because of girlfriends, boy friends, group membership and hobbies.

When we marry and have children, our concept of love again changes and expands. Our eyes are opened to what our parents went through with us.

When our parents pass away, our qualities of love increase, grief, empathy, sympathy, are more fullblown.

With age we add a new dimension to our idea of love, which is endless and expands without limitations.

The way we expand concepts will give us a quality of experience. Those who expand hatred will never know love like those who practice compassion, and kindness.

The way you expand your concepts will be the way you feel about life. Watch out where you are going with your qualities.

THINGS TO THINK ABOUT

The best salesman knows that a bright, flashy, quick, gimmick, is best to win you over. The beat of the music should quickly hook you. The car, or clothing design should have an immediate appeal. The movie, a fast action, loud colorful plot. Food is prepared for convenience of speed and taste, not for nutrition or health.

That which appeals to the senses easily, has a tendency of losing its enjoyment in a short period of time, so one fad is traded for another.

But outside the cultural fads of quick appeal, exists a different dimension. The dimension of learning to steadily enjoy the same things over again, with a new insight.

Beethoven, Mozart, Bach, offer a music that is never outdated or limited. Authors such as, Albert Schweizer, Ralph Emerson, and Walt Whitman, have written material that doesn't get old. The more you read the newer it gets.

That which you slowly learn to enjoy will enhance your life ten fold.

In a fast moving culture, the ego learns to quickly accept fads, and to emotionally react without thinking. The deeper essence of your being, neglected. Take time to control the ego and become the observer, then each moment becomes an experience in fully living.

Personal substance is like good literature - its worth having.

THINGS TO THINK ABOUT

What value have you gained because of the problem experiences that you have lived through? How much money would you take to sell the knowledge of life you have gained in connection with trouble experiences?

Would you like to be stranded in a boat with someone who has lived a luxurious, pampered life, or with someone who has endured hardships? Which one would be the best leader?

Life with its problems give us knowledge, a worth that cannot be found in a book, or bought with money.

With a positive approach, most problems can be used beneficially. Be strategic with your observation of a problem. See the benefits they have, use them, ride with the energy they offer, like a surfur would a wave. Give them size and dimension. Schedule time to think and plan. Never allow yourself to be pessimistic, think of problems as a way to temper the spirit. With time, age and problems, you can mold the will power, and test your life theories. You gain much more out of life with problems, than without them.

THINGS TO THINK ABOUT

Many people have developed negative thinking as a defense to protect themselves from stress. They have developed a muscular tension that is constant. Because of their way of thinking they are always unbalanced, the center of focus cannot be put into the hips. They are unable to do the exercises in this book. They should learn what they have done to themselves, and learn to relax and become positive, then the power of the body will function properly and they will be able to do the exercises.

Do to the fast paced stressful society about one out of every thirty people cannot do the exercises in this book.

*****

Many people look at discipline with fear. They think in terms of avoiding it. Discipline means, ridgid control, an arid, dull way of being.

But discipline has its value. With discipline you can control eating habits, alcohol, cigarettes, and repattern unwanted behavior traits.

The mind always wants, its never satisfied, the body seeks pleasure, it wants more entertainment, food, comforts.

Give up discipline and serve the minds wants, and bodys pleasure, and you give up freedom.

Discipline brings order and freedom to your life. Discipline is freedom.

THINGS TO THINK ABOUT

Thought changes constantly, self image alters, the ego rearranges itself. What part of you observes all of this? It is the part of your mind that is just pure awareness, the witness, the absolute self. This is the calm, serene natural property, that is never disturbed, it is untouched, always calm. Regardless of what happens, in the external world or what thoughts occur to you, this part of your nature does not ever change.

When you focus attention and become the witness, or observe, you can watch the ego, and events with composure, you keep a mental distance. By watching your ego objectively and questioning it, you learn to see, hear, and think on a larger scale. Openness, and mindfulness will prevail, instead of the ego games of keeping up with the Joneses, imitating, wearing the social mask, and need for approval. Tension, and aggression are dealt with in a controlled, effective manner. The ego doesn't uncontrollably attract you emotionally into a problem as easily.

Without mental neutrality you follow the ego as it adjusts, balances, changes, and reshapes, its image. As an observer you control the ego, monitor thoughts, and become the master of your life. The ego thinks it knows everything, and is the master, but this is only an act. The observer is really the master.

Quietly observe your own thinking, keep a mental distance, and build a positive belief system. Take over your own life, determine your own emotions, and physical powers. Remember, nobody gets you upset, but yourself. Events don't irritate you, you do. Job pressure, problems, and strain, are terms the ego uses to guide you into irritation and depression.

Stress and change are the river of life in which you are swimming. You cannot change or eliminate problems, so you must improve your own reactions to the way you handle a problem.

Control, happiness, efficiency, adaptability, comes from within. Its up to you to keep everything in its proper perspective, to relate to the world as a holistic person rather than a fragmented individual.

BECOME THE OBSERVER, QUESTION THE EGO, AND UTILIZE POSITIVE VALUES.

USE THESE CONCEPTS IN YOUR HUMAN EQUATION AND YOUR QUALITY OF LIFE WILL CONTINUALLY ELEVATE.

THINGS TO THINK ABOUT

Competition is healthy, fun and beneficial in many ways, but there is a point where the deeper meaning of life is lost. Within the dilemma of sports young children, backed by parents, bitterly compete to win. Parents argue with referees, one side stays mad at the other. Bad feelings grow and multiply. Win at all costs, be number one, take over, even if it means degrading somebody else. Get tough and negative.

A game never exists as an isolated moment separate from real life. Sports and games that people play are real. Sports are often the corner stone that teach young children how to win and lose in life.

Being a champion with physical technique alone can be detremental to someones life. Negative attitudes and childish impulses, are often encouraged in the battle to win. In many cases anger, frustration and egotism are supported and clapped for. Primitive impulses are allowed expression with honor. Spectators and participants get lost in the game of play and lose their perspective on life.

Enthusiasm and the spirit to win is very important to cultivate, and can be done in a positive constructive way, but too often adults glorify the fact that they have a short fuse, (get mad easily), and young children learn to take pride in getting upset, and angry. Aggression with anger is respected.

Sports is a physical tool, that can be used to teach perseverance, psychological endurance and strength of character. Maximum efficiency is found, when the mind, body and spirit are in unity. When the mind and body are properly balanced and integrated. When the spirit to win takes a positive, progressive direction.

Sports have been used to train the body, and the training of the mind has been left up to the class room, the training of the spirit neglected. The wise superior athlete will learn to unify mind, body and spirit, he will combine ethics with sports.

Ethics with sports offers a high level of performance because self control improves with the ability to learn.

Maximum efficiency is found with a calm mind, and with the spirit of discipline.

The key to quick accurate body response, and mental clarity is found in benevolence.

When an athlete trains with negative attitudes, they give their self control up to the score board, the audience, and to the opposite team. This way of behavior is transfered into daily life.

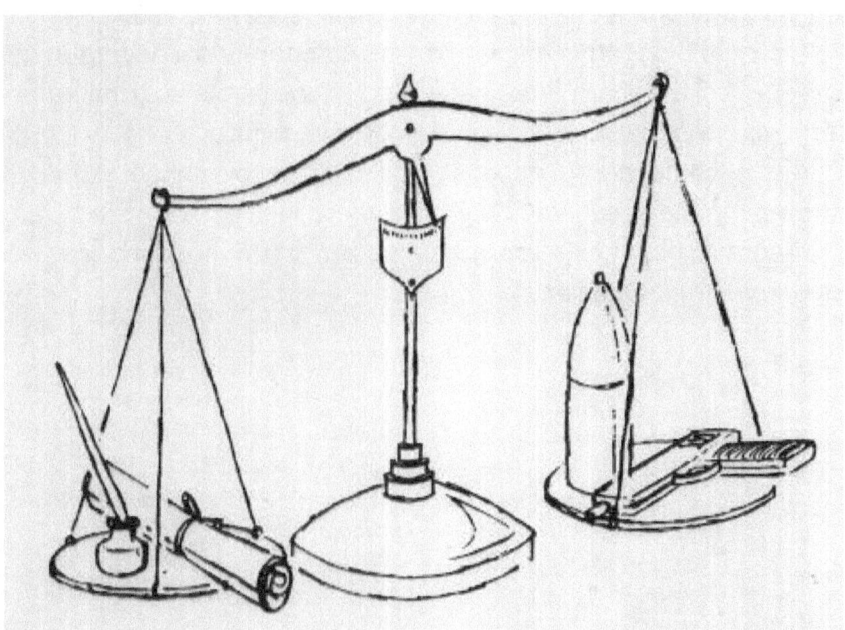

War, crime - problems like these are solved by elevating the level of consciousness.

THINGS TO THINK ABOUT

A dog in the streets learns to avoid cars. The ability to adjust to the hazards of the environment determine survival.

To hold thoughts of anger, can be compared to standing in the street with the dogs that are not willing to cooperate with the traffic. You will get run over because of your own thinking.

To become angry because you are run over then stand up stronger in the street, will only invite more injury.

Learn to blend with the traffic, the process of handling life with anger will run you over.

THE MARTIAL ARTS

Traditionally the martial arts are dedicated to the building of better character and the improvement of society.

The founder of Judo, Dr. Jigoro Kano, had a second maxim of Judo which was: "Build society by harmonious cooperation with others." This is a basic way of being that is learned in Judo training.

During Judo training, subtle mental changes take place. One learns to quickly adjust and blend in harmony with the attackers strengths and weaknesses. From this information one learns about his own thinking, and reactions. A world of knowledge takes place within seconds, never to be repeated exactly the same way again.

The historical foundations of Karate emphasized the development of the mind, body and spirit. The traditional spirit of Karate, is to understand one's self better each day, and move onward toward life, by cultivating a positive mind.

The greatest gift is the cultivated mind. A cultivated mind is accurate with insight, and the intuitive senses are improved. One learns to respond with a natural innocence, which is quick and strong.

*****

By 1970, I had spent ten years in tournament competition and resolved to keep up my training, but I also wanted to share the finer benefits of the Martial Arts with other people. To accomplish this goal, I founded the Kenju Studio so that the philosophical concepts of the martial arts would be emphasized, practiced, and improved.

In 1972, I started to teach special self improvement programs. This has developed into stress and management seminars.

In recent years, I have made many new discoveries in relationship to the mind and body. The Human Equation is a condensed version of my discoveries and previous martial arts training.

The following metaphysical techniques are those I have used to help me win in competition. These concepts will, hopefully, help those of you who are in competition.

JUDO

During Judo training, keep the concentration down through the body. Imagine water flowing through the legs. Breathe deeply and imagine the breath exhaling downward. Don't concentrate on the opponents hands or on the upper Judo Gi. Be at one with the moment so you intuitively react. Because of the eyes, we pay more attention to the front of our body. Close the eyes, tune into the sides of your body and the back. Be circular, place emphasis on the whole body. Don't put the techniques into words try to make the throw a feeling, a natural blend.

As you project downward, extend outwardly. Like a triangle, have a powerful base. The more energy you have the bigger the base.

Imagine the opponent's body where you would like it to be, then you can throw them just because of the mental feeling.

Learn to see Judo in all of life, then your training will really be of value.

Judo is one of the most beneficial ways of learning about life and yourself, because it trains the body to understand life in an intuitive way and the mind in a blending harmonious way.

When you warm up the body, include the idea of projecting downward through the body. As you move the feet, build up excitment, energy, and then express this energy with kicks. Don't physically kick without the spirit of enthusiasm. The power for the technique comes from the hips, this is also your balancing point. Muscles should be relaxed and focused in harmony at the same time.

Work out with everyone regardless of rank, because each person has a movement, a timing, that nobody else can give you.

Use the form movements to repattern the body and mind. Slow movement will pattern the nervous system very fast. Intensity and concentration should always be included in Kata practice.

Don't avoid tournaments, and work hard, the hardest path is the easiest one.

Everyone reaches a barrior, a mental wall, where they want to quit or take it easy. At this point its your attitude that will determine what you do. Your decision at this moment determines if your a champion or not.

Adjust your thinking, so you will work out even though you prefer not to, and you will be a champion in about four years.

Judo, Karate, and Aikido techniques all have principles that are closely related. By studying one you. study elements of the others. Instead of exclusively practicing one system or style of self defense, I strongly recommend that you understudy all the arts.

CONCLUSION

The Preamble of the Constitution says: "We the People of the United States, in Order to form a more perfect Union, establish Justice. . ." Justice is established through the character of the people.

The Preamble also says ". . . insure domestic Tranquility..." This is done by teaching the powers of positive thinking to young children.

And the Preamble also says ". . . provide for the common defense . . ." The best defense is an offense, the offense is in the form of cultivating the spirit of elevating the quality of life. The Preamble goes on ". . . promote the general Welfare, and secure the Blessing of Liberty to ourselves and our Posterity. . ." This can best be done with wisdom and values.

Freedom must be learned. Mental serenity and inner tranquility are not given to anyone free. They must work for these qualities.

We give freedom to ourselves by understanding how to best use our mind and body potentials.

As the individual elevates so does society.

In a free society, liberty and the pursuit of happiness is based upon the wisdom of the human consciousness. The level of consciousness is transferred into public policy and life style. Freedom is not given, it is earned by elevating the consciousness toward higher ideals and the building of character.

Values x Belief system = OUR quality of life.

Values x Belief System = Quality of Life

www.ingramcontent.com/pod-product-compliance
Lightning Source LLC
Chambersburg PA
CBHW050427290526
45786CB00003B/1428